I0436589

PREDICTIVE ANALYTICS FOR CUSTOMER BEHAVIOR:

USING AI TO PREDICT CUSTOMER BEHAVIOR TRENDS HELPS IN MAKING DATA-DRIVEN MARKETING DECISIONS

BY

HENRY E. PARKINS

COPYRIGHT PAGE

TABLE OF CONTENTS

4

INTRODUCTION

In the vast landscape of modern business, the ability to understand and anticipate customer behavior stands as the bedrock of success. Enter the realm of "Predictive Analytics for Customer Behavior," a comprehensive exploration that unravels the intricate tapestry of predictive analytics and its pivotal role in deciphering the complexities of consumer actions and preferences.

Definition and Explanation of Predictive Analytics

Predictive analytics represents the quintessence of data-driven decision-making. It encompasses a set of

6

statistical techniques and methodologies that mine historical data, identify patterns, and generate insights to predict future outcomes or behaviors. Through the lens of customer behavior, predictive analytics serves as a powerful tool to forecast, anticipate, and comprehend the actions and preferences of consumers.

Importance of Predictive Analytics in Understanding Customer Behavior

At the heart of successful marketing strategies lies a deep understanding of customer behavior. Predictive analytics plays an instrumental role by providing organizations with foresight into the potential actions, preferences, and inclinations of their customers. This predictive prowess enables businesses to tailor offerings, personalize experiences, and optimize strategies, creating a resonance with customers that transcends mere satisfaction, fostering lasting relationships.

Evolution of Predictive Analytics in Marketing

The evolution of predictive analytics in marketing is a testament to the ever-expanding horizons of technological innovation. From humble beginnings to its present state, predictive analytics has evolved into an indispensable asset, empowering marketers with actionable insights derived from vast

8

troves of data. This evolution has enabled a shift from reactive to proactive strategies, allowing businesses to anticipate and adapt to changing consumer behaviors in real-time.

As we journey through the chapters of this book, we will delve into the fundamental principles, methodologies, and practical applications of predictive analytics for customer behavior analysis. From understanding the foundational aspects of consumer behavior to exploring sophisticated predictive models and ethical considerations, this comprehensive guide aims to equip marketers, analysts, and decision-makers with the tools and insights to navigate the dynamic realm of customer behavior prediction.

Each chapter offers an in-depth exploration, unveiling the intricacies, opportunities, and challenges associated with predictive analytics. By the book's conclusion, readers will gain a holistic understanding of predictive analytics' pivotal role in deciphering customer behavior and its profound implications for shaping the future of marketing strategies.

10

CHAPTER 1

FOUNDATIONS OF CUSTOMER BEHAVIOR ANALYSIS

Understanding consumer behavior forms the cornerstone of effective marketing strategies. This chapter delves into the foundational aspects of deciphering customer behavior, exploring data sources, collection methods, and the pivotal role of data in predictive analysis.

Understanding Consumer Behavior

Consumer behavior is a multifaceted study encompassing the various

11

actions, needs, motivations, and decision-making processes of individuals or groups when purchasing or interacting with products, services, or brands. Exploring the psychology behind consumer actions helps unravel patterns, preferences, and the influences shaping purchasing behaviors. Factors such as social, psychological, and cultural aspects play pivotal roles in shaping consumer choices and preferences.

Data Sources and Collection Methods for Customer Behavior

a. *Transactional Data:* Purchase history, sales records, and customer transactions provide valuable

12

insights into past behaviors, preferences, and buying patterns.

b. *Online Behavior and Interactions:* Data collected from website visits, clickstreams, browsing history, and online interactions offer insights into customer preferences, interests, and engagement levels.

c. *Surveys and Feedback:* Direct feedback and survey responses from customers provide qualitative data, offering nuanced insights into preferences, opinions, and sentiments.

d. *Social Media and User-generated Content:* Analysis of social media activity, comments, reviews, and user-generated content yields valuable information about customer perceptions, trends, and sentiments.

e. IoT Devices and Sensors: Data collected from IoT devices and sensors offer real-time behavioral insights, such as usage patterns, location-based information, and product interactions.

Exploring the Role of Data in Predictive Analysis

Data serves as the lifeblood of predictive analysis. The abundance and quality of data determine the accuracy and reliability of predictive models. In predictive analysis, historical data is used to identify patterns, correlations, and trends that form the basis for forecasting future behaviors. The role of data in

14

predictive analysis is to train models, validate predictions, and continuously refine the accuracy of predictions by incorporating new data inputs.

Understanding consumer behavior through data-driven insights lays the groundwork for predictive analytics. By comprehending the various sources of data and their implications in predictive analysis, businesses can harness this information to develop accurate predictive models that anticipate and respond to customer behavior effectively.

CHAPTER 2

TECHNIQUES AND MODELS FOR PREDICTIVE ANALYTICS

Predictive analytics encompasses a range of powerful techniques and models that enable businesses to anticipate and understand customer behavior. This chapter elucidates on distinct methodologies tailored for customer behavior prediction, encompassing regression analysis, classification models, time series analysis, and clustering algorithms.

Regression Analysis for Predicting Customer Behavior

Regression analysis is a statistical technique used to examine the relationship between a dependent variable and one or more independent variables. In customer behavior prediction, regression models help quantify the impact of various factors on consumer actions. By analyzing historical data, regression models can predict future behaviors, such as purchase likelihood based on variables like demographics, past purchases, or website interactions.

Classification Models in Customer Segmentation

Classification models, including decision trees, random forests, and support vector machines, are employed for customer segmentation. These models categorize customers into distinct groups based on shared characteristics or behaviors. By assigning individuals to specific segments, businesses can tailor marketing strategies, personalize experiences, and optimize campaigns to meet the unique needs of each group.

Time Series Analysis for Trend Forecasting

18

Time series analysis focuses on studying data points collected over consecutive time intervals to uncover patterns and trends. In predicting customer behavior, time series models forecast future trends, preferences, or purchase patterns based on historical time-stamped data. By analyzing temporal patterns, businesses can anticipate cyclic behaviors or seasonal trends, enabling proactive strategies and resource allocation.

Clustering Algorithms for Behavioral Segmentation

Clustering algorithms, such as k-means clustering or hierarchical clustering, group customers based on similar behaviors or attributes.

19

These algorithms analyze multivariate data to identify distinct segments within the customer base. Behavioral segmentation derived from clustering aids in understanding diverse customer preferences, enabling targeted and personalized marketing strategies for each segment.

Each predictive analytics technique plays a distinct role in deciphering customer behavior. While regression analysis quantifies relationships between variables, classification models segment customers based on characteristics, and time series analysis predicts temporal patterns. Clustering algorithms, on the other hand, facilitate behavioral segmentation, empowering businesses to tailor strategies

20

aligned with diverse customer preferences and behaviors. Understanding and leveraging these techniques are pivotal in crafting effective predictive models for understanding and predicting customer behavior.

CHAPTER 3

IMPLEMENTING PREDICTIVE ANALYTICS IN MARKETING

Harnessing the power of predictive analytics in marketing is pivotal to create impactful and targeted strategies that resonate with customers. This chapter delves into the practical applications of predictive analytics, showcasing how businesses can leverage it to personalize experiences, customize marketing strategies, and make real-time decisions based on predictive insights.

Leveraging Predictive Analytics in Personalization

Predictive analytics enables personalized experiences by leveraging insights derived from customer data. By understanding past behaviors and preferences, businesses can personalize interactions, product recommendations, and content delivery. Tailored messaging and offerings resonate more effectively with customers, fostering stronger connections and driving engagement and loyalty.

Customizing Marketing Strategies Using Predictive Models

Predictive models serve as guiding tools for customizing marketing strategies. These models analyze historical data to forecast future behaviors, enabling marketers to optimize their approaches. By understanding what customers are likely to do next, businesses can adapt their marketing efforts, allocate resources efficiently, and design campaigns that align with predicted preferences and behaviors.

Real-time Decision Making Based on Predictive Insights

The real power of predictive analytics lies in its ability to offer actionable insights in real time. Businesses equipped with predictive models can make informed decisions

24

promptly. By analyzing incoming data streams, predictive models provide up-to-date insights, allowing businesses to adjust strategies on-the-fly, seize opportunities, and mitigate risks as they emerge.

Implementing predictive analytics in marketing isn't just about making predictions; it's about leveraging these insights to craft personalized experiences, refine strategies, and make informed, timely decisions that resonate with customers.

The successful integration of predictive analytics in marketing empowers businesses to deliver hyper-personalized experiences, tailor marketing strategies, and make agile decisions in a dynamic market landscape. As we explore the

25

practical applications of predictive analytics in marketing, it becomes evident that leveraging these insights isn't merely a choice but a necessity for businesses striving to thrive in a competitive environment.

CHAPTER 4

APPLICATIONS AND CASE STUDIES

Predictive analytics transcends industry boundaries, offering invaluable insights and applications across diverse sectors. This chapter examines prominent applications of predictive analytics in various industries, showcasing how it revolutionizes strategies and drives impactful decision-making. Additionally, it presents successful case studies highlighting the effectiveness of predictive models in different domains.

Predictive Analytics in E-commerce and Retail

In the realm of e-commerce and retail, predictive analytics serves as a game-changer. By analyzing past purchase behaviors, browsing patterns, and customer interactions, businesses predict future buying trends, personalize product recommendations, and optimize pricing strategies. Case studies demonstrate how e-commerce giants leverage predictive models to enhance user experience, improve inventory management, and boost sales through targeted marketing.

28

Predictive Models in Financial Services and Banking

Financial institutions harness predictive analytics to mitigate risks, detect fraud, and personalize financial services. By analyzing transactional data and customer behaviors, banks tailor financial products, predict creditworthiness, and identify potential risks. Case examples illustrate how predictive models enable personalized banking experiences, optimize loan approvals, and enhance fraud detection mechanisms.

Predictive Analysis in Healthcare and Telecommunications

In the healthcare sector, predictive analytics aids in disease prediction, patient outcomes, and resource allocation. By analyzing patient data and medical history, healthcare providers predict health risks, personalize treatment plans, and optimize healthcare delivery. Telecommunications companies utilize predictive models to anticipate network traffic, improve service quality, and forecast customer churn. Case studies highlight the efficacy of predictive analytics in improving patient care, optimizing network performance, and driving business growth.

Successful Implementations and Case Examples

Explore real-world success stories across industries that exemplify the efficacy of predictive analytics. Witness how companies leverage predictive models to achieve tangible results, including increased revenue, improved customer satisfaction, and streamlined operations. Case examples showcase the transformative impact of predictive analytics on businesses, fostering growth, and enabling data-driven decision-making.

Through these applications and case studies, it becomes evident that

31

predictive analytics isn't merely a tool but a catalyst for innovation, empowering industries to make informed decisions, personalize experiences, and drive success in an increasingly data-centric world.

CHAPTER 5

ETHICAL CONSIDERATIONS AND CHALLENGES

The ethical implications surrounding the use of predictive analytics in understanding customer behavior are critical aspects that warrant careful consideration. This chapter explores the ethical dimensions and challenges inherent in employing predictive analytics for customer behavior analysis.

Privacy and Ethical Implications of Predictive Analytics

The pervasive use of customer data in predictive analytics raises concerns regarding individual privacy and ethical considerations. The extensive collection, analysis, and utilization of personal data could potentially infringe upon privacy rights. Addressing these concerns requires businesses to uphold stringent data privacy standards, ensure transparency in data usage, and obtain explicit consent from individuals for data collection and analysis.

Challenges in Data Quality and Bias in Predictive Modeling

Data quality and biases pose significant challenges in predictive modeling. Inaccurate or incomplete datasets can lead to flawed predictions and biased outcomes. Biases within data, such as historical biases or sampling biases, can perpetuate discriminatory predictions, impacting decision-making processes. To mitigate these challenges, businesses must ensure data accuracy, minimize biases in algorithms, and implement fairness and accountability measures in predictive models.

Overcoming Ethical Challenges in Customer Behavior Analysis

Overcoming ethical challenges in customer behavior analysis necessitates proactive measures and ethical frameworks. Implementing stringent governance policies, conducting regular audits, and fostering a culture of ethical awareness are crucial. Embracing transparency in predictive analytics processes and fostering accountability helps in building trust among customers while ensuring responsible and ethical use of their data.

Navigating the ethical landscape of predictive analytics in customer behavior analysis demands a delicate balance between leveraging data-driven insights and safeguarding individual rights. By adopting ethical frameworks and addressing inherent challenges, businesses can uphold ethical standards, build trust with customers, and foster a responsible approach to predictive analytics.

CHAPTER 6

FUTURE TRENDS AND INNOVATIONS

The landscape of predictive analytics for understanding customer behavior continues to evolve rapidly, driven by technological advancements and innovative methodologies. This chapter delves into the future trends and anticipated innovations that are poised to reshape the realm of predictive analytics.

Advancements in Predictive Analytics Technologies

The future of predictive analytics is marked by advancements in technology, including enhanced algorithms, more sophisticated models, and faster processing capabilities. Predictive analytics tools will evolve to handle larger and more complex datasets efficiently. Advancements in data visualization and interpretability will empower businesses to extract actionable insights more seamlessly from their data.

Integration of AI and Machine Learning in Predictive Modeling

The integration of artificial intelligence (AI) and machine learning techniques will revolutionize predictive modeling. AI-driven models will become more adept at understanding intricate patterns in data, enabling more accurate predictions. The utilization of deep learning algorithms will enhance predictive capabilities, enabling systems to analyze unstructured data types, such as images and text, for richer insights into customer behavior.

Anticipated Impacts and Innovations in Customer Behavior Prediction

The future holds significant transformations in how businesses predict and understand customer behavior. The adoption of predictive analytics will become more pervasive across industries, enabling hyper-personalization and highly

40

targeted marketing strategies. Predictive models will evolve to predict not only behavior but also emotions and intent, fostering deeper customer relationships and enhancing customer experiences.

The convergence of these future trends will empower businesses to unlock new frontiers in customer behavior prediction. Advancements in technology and methodologies will revolutionize predictive analytics, enabling businesses to anticipate customer needs, personalize interactions, and make data-driven decisions with unprecedented accuracy.

As predictive analytics continues to evolve, businesses that embrace these innovations will gain a

41

competitive edge, driving innovation, and setting new benchmarks in understanding and predicting customer behavior. The future of predictive analytics promises a transformative era, redefining how businesses connect with their customers and drive sustainable growth through data-driven insights.

CHAPTER 7

CONCLUSION

As we conclude our exploration into "Predictive Analytics for Customer Behavior," it becomes evident that predictive analytics serves as a catalyst in understanding and anticipating the complex nuances of customer behavior. This concluding chapter recaps the significant role of predictive analytics, summarizes key insights, and reflects on the future outlook of predictive analytics in shaping marketing strategies.

Recap of the Role of Predictive Analytics in Customer Behavior Understanding

Predictive analytics acts as a beacon illuminating the path to comprehending customer behavior. It enables businesses to decipher intricate patterns, anticipate preferences, and forecast behaviors. By harnessing predictive models, businesses gain insights that empower them to personalize experiences, tailor strategies, and make informed decisions that resonate with customers on a deeper level.

Summary of Key Takeaways and Insights

Throughout this journey, we've uncovered critical insights. From understanding the foundations of customer behavior analysis to exploring advanced techniques and ethical considerations, the key takeaways emphasize the transformative potential of predictive analytics. The significance of data-driven decision-making, the necessity of ethical considerations, and the power of innovation in shaping the future of marketing strategies stand out as pivotal insights.

Final Thoughts on the Future Outlook of Predictive Analytics in Marketing Strategies

Looking ahead, the future of predictive analytics in marketing strategies appears promising and transformative. The integration of cutting-edge technologies, such as AI and machine learning, will elevate predictive models to unprecedented levels of accuracy and sophistication. The future outlook emphasizes a shift towards hyper-personalization, real-time decision-making, and an unwavering commitment to ethical practices.

In conclusion, "Predictive Analytics for Customer Behavior" stands at the intersection of innovation and understanding. The insights gained through predictive analytics not only illuminate customer behaviors but also pave the way for strategic advancements in marketing. The future outlook promises a dynamic landscape where businesses equipped with predictive analytics will have the ability to forge deeper connections, drive exceptional customer experiences, and chart new territories of success in an ever-evolving marketplace. As businesses embrace these insights and innovations, they are poised to thrive, setting new benchmarks in customer-centric strategies powered by predictive analytics.

OTHER BOOKS BY THE AUTHOR

USINESS ETHICS AND CORPORATE SOCIALRESPONSIBILITY: CREATING A PURPOSE-DRIVEN COMPANY

SIDE HUSTLE HANDBOOK: EARNING EXTRA INCOME FOR FINANCIAL INDEPENDENCE

A GUIDE TO TRACKING CRYPTOCURRENCY WHALES: SCALE-UP YOUR CRYPTOCURRENCY PORTFOLIOS (10,000X)

BUILDING RESILIENCE AND EMOTIONAL INTELLIGENCE

INVESTOR'S GUIDE: THE POWER OF FUNDAMENTAL ANALYSIS OF FOREX TRADING

WHAT BILLIONAIRES DOES TO BECOME WEALTHY: UNDERSTANDING THE GAME

THE RULE OF THE BILLIONAIRES

DISCOVER SELF DEVELOPMENT BOOKS

THE AI AUTHOR'S GUIDE: CRAFTING YOUR BOOK WITH ARTIFICIAL INTELLIGENCE

Note Page 5...........................Date................

Use this page for all writing during reading or study.

Note Page 5..........................Date................

Use this page for all writing during reading or study.

Note Page 5...........................Date................

Use this page for all writing during reading or study.

Note Page 5..........................Date...............

Use this page for all writing during reading or study.

Note Page 5...........................Date................

Use this page for all writing during reading or study.

Note Page 5...........................Date.................

Use this page for all writing during reading or study.

Note Page 5...........................Date................

Use this page for all writing during reading or study.

Note Page 5...........................Date................

Use this page for all writing during reading or study.

Note Page 5...........................Date................

Use this page for all writing during reading or study.

Note Page 5...........................Date................

Use this page for all writing during reading or study.

Note Page 5...........................Date................

Use this page for all writing during reading or study.

Note Page 5.........................Date...............

Use this page for all writing during reading or study.

Note Page 5...........................Date................

Use this page for all writing during reading or study.

Note Page 5...........................Date.................

Use this page for all writing during reading or study.

Note Page 5...........................Date................

Use this page for all writing during reading or study.

Note Page 5...........................Date................

Use this page for all writing during reading or study.

Note Page 5...........................Date................

Use this page for all writing during reading or study.

Note Page 5..........................Date...............

Use this page for all writing during reading or study.

Note Page 5...........................Date................

Use this page for all writing during reading or study.

Note Page 5..........................Date................

Use this page for all writing during reading or study.

Note Page 5...........................Date................

Use this page for all writing during reading or study.

Note Page 5...........................Date................

Use this page for all writing during reading or study.

Note Page 5...........................Date................

Use this page for all writing during reading or study.

Note Page 5..........................Date................

Use this page for all writing during reading or study.

Note Page 5..........................Date................

Use this page for all writing during reading or study.

Note Page 5.........................Date...............

Use this page for all writing during reading or study.

www.ingramcontent.com/pod-product-compliance
Lightning Source LLC
Chambersburg PA
CBHW071213290526
45796CB00008B/230